ART AND HISTORY
OF
JORDAN

Introduction by
RAMI G. KHOURI

Text by
FRANCESCA CASULE

BONECHI

ART AND HISTORY OF JORDAN

Conceptual project and publishing: Casa Editrice Bonechi
Iconographic research: Giovanna Magi
Graphic project and layout: Sonia Gottardo
Editing: Simonetta Giorgi
Videographics: Laura Settesoldi

Texts by Rami G. Khouri *and* Francesca Casule
Captions: Giovanna Magi
Translation by Erika Pauli
Plans on pages 34 and 88 by Studio Grafico Daniela Mariani, Pistoia
Map of Jordan: Jordan Geographical Center

ISBN 88-8029-416-4

* * *

INDEX

HISTORICAL INTRODUCTION

Deeply etched into Jordan's kaleidoscopic landscape of green highlands, stark deserts and lush valleys is the oldest and most exciting spectacle on Earth: the uninterrupted development of human culture, art and civilisation since its origins in the days of Stone Age hunter-gatherers, always reflecting man's adaptation to different climatic/environmental zones.

Along the west of the country, the warm and well watered Jordan Rift Valley reaches a depth of over 400 metres below sea level at the Dead Sea the lowest spot on Earth with its southern terminus at the tropical town/port of Aqaba on the Red Sea. Immediately east of the valley, and 800-2000 metres above it, the 20-40-kilometre-deep spine of cooler, wetter highlands runs down the entire length of the country. This rainfed farming zone has always included the land's leading population centres, such as Petra, Jerash, Amman, Madaba, Gadara, and Kerak. East of the highlands is the vast, semi-arid, steppe-like eastern desert ("el-badia" in Arabic) with its "bedou" inhabitants (the "bedouin" in English). For thousands of years, they have mastered this challenging environment by practising a lifestyle of nomadic livestocking, following fixed seasonal routes among known water and forage sources.

Throughout history, the nomadic bedou and the settled villagers and town-dwellers have had a mutually beneficial and symbiotic relationship. The bedou trade animal products (meat, wool, woven rugs, dehydrated yoghourt) for manufactured or imported goods (sugar, weapons, clothes, wood or metal utensils) and agricultural produce.

From at least 5000 years ago, when the King's Highway (mentioned by that name in the book of Genesis) was an important north/south road in the time of Abraham and his nephew Lot, the land of Jordan has been strategically important for regional and even world powers, for three reasons: its water, fertile land and mineral resources (bitumen, salt, copper), its strategic value as a buffer or frontier zone between ancient civilisations (such as Egypt, Assyria, Persia, Greece, Rome, Byzantium, and Islam) and its status as a vital link on the ancient world's leading trade routes (including the spice, silk and incense routes).

This combination of varied terrains, lifestyles, economic systems and natural assets meant that Jordan has been continuously inhabited since the pre-dawn of human history. Big powers that remained in control for centuries (Assyria, Egypt, Rome, Byzantium, Islam) changed the cultural landscape in major ways. Some cultures (Edom, Moab, Ammon, Nabataea) reflected indigenous peoples who established their own political entities in Jordan. Other cultures (India, southern Arabia, Persia) did not physically control the area, but their cultural and artistic influences penetrated the land and people of Jordan.

An important recurring theme in the art, culture and history of Jordan is the interplay and synthesis of traditions from different sources. For example, temples in Jerash and other Roman era cities are usually located on hilltops, following a long-standing Middle Eastern tradition of siting cultic or religious facilities on high places. In the Islamic period fresco art of 7th Century Qasr Amra or the architecture of Qasr Kharana, one can clearly see traces of Byzantine, Persian and even Indian influences. At Petra, the major Nabataean rock-cut monuments could well have been designed by Hellenistic architects, and many funerary obelisks at Petra recall the influence of Egypt.

The earliest evidence of human activity in Jordan is stone tools from Paleolithic period hunter-gatherers and perhaps also some rock art depicting animal or hunting scenes (circa 1.2 million years ago to 17,000 BC). Around 17,000 BC, as the climate became drier and large herds of wild animals dwindled, hunter-gatherers learned to domesticate animals and cultivate plants. Small groups of people settled down into seasonal camps with simple shelters that soon evolved into huts, proper houses, hamlets, and finally into year-round villages.

The transition from hunter-gatherer to settled villager produced the Neolithic (new stone age) culture in the period 8000-4500 BC. Ain Ghazal, Basta and Beidha are three excavated Neolithic sites that can be easily visited in Jordan. In the Chalcolithic ("copper-stone") Period around 4500-3200 BC, the inhabitants of large agricultural villages, who had already mastered pottery making, first made and used copper arrowheads, blades, axes and other metal tools. The Early Bronze Age (3000-2900 BC) witnessed the development of small walled towns and fortified cities with thick stone walls and defensive towers, such as those excavated at Bab ed-Dhraa, Zerakhon, Jawa and Lehhun. These people exchanged goods and cultural influences with nearby civilisations in Mesopotamia, Assyria, Egypt and Mycenae.

Jordan's urban development continued in the Middle and Late Bronze Ages (1900-1200 BC), as ever larger fortified towns (Tell Sa'idiyyeh, Pella) developed strong trading links with Anatolia, Egypt and the Aegean. Cylinder seals from this period depict an assortment of Egyptian, Syrian and Babylonian-style deities and motifs.

During the transition from the Bronze Age to the Iron Age around 1200 BC Jordan witnessed the birth of small kingdoms, including Edom, Moab and Ammon, which had attributes of small nation-states. These lasted for about 600 years during the Iron Age either as independent kingdoms or under the successive political influence of Assyria, Babylonia and Persia. They left a rich legacy of ceramics, stone statues, metal objects, jewellery and scripts, from sites such as Sahab, Amman, Tell Safut, Dhiban, Tell Mazar and Tell Deir Alla. During the last two centuries of the Iron Age in Jordan (539-333 BC), the area was under the political dominance of the Persian (Achaemenid) Empire.

When the army of Alexander the Great swept into Syria and Jordan after 332 BC, they brought with them the powerful Greco-Roman culture that would dominate the region for nearly a millennium. Qasr el-Abed (Iraq el-Emir), west of Amman, is the best preserved of the few Hellenistic era monuments in Jordan.

The Nabataean Kingdom had started to take shape in south Jordan by this time, as nomadic Nabataean Arabs in northern Arabia and southern Jordan gradually settled in south Jordan in the 6th and 5th Centuries BC and displaced the remnants of the Edomites. By the second century BC the Nabataean capital city at Petra was already internationally renowned for its beauty and wealth. Today, Petra's mountain-ringed basin with over 800 monuments, most of which were carved out of the pink and cinnamon Nubian sandstone, is a sparkling synthesis of natural beauty, Nabataean monumental art, and the fusion of indigenous Nabataean art with imported Greco-Roman, Egyptian and Assyrian traditions.

For at least 400 years, until they fell under Roman control in 106 AD, the Nabataeans built a wealthy kingdom on the basis of their trading skills, their political agility and their technological capabilities. They used diplomacy to avoid warfare and maintain open trading frontiers, exchanging commodities from Asia and Southern Arabia (incense, myrrh and spices) with merchants in the Mediterranean Basin.

The Nabataeans left few original written records other than funerary inscriptions written in a Nabataean script derived from the Aramaic script that was the lingua franca of the Near East in the late 1st Millennium BC. Nabataean art and technology, though, are well attested, especially their ceramic and hydrological skills. Nabataean statues speak eloquently of the elegance that sculptors could derive from a piece of stone perhaps because in their nomadic days they had represented their gods as easily manufactured and transportable stone blocs. These initially unadorned stone blocs soon took on slits that were simple schematic eyes and a nose; later, perhaps due to the influence of Greco-Roman culture, the Nabataeans adorned their deities with full facial features, and finally represented them in full three dimensional human form. A fish goddess and a statue of Victory carrying the Zodiac on her shoulders (from the temple at Khirbet Tannur) are classic examples of the synthesis of Nabataean and Hellenistic culture. This is also seen in busts of Dushara, the most important Nabataean male deity, who is equated with Dionyses.

The Nabataeans were master potters, known for their distinctive, very thin and highly decorated pottery. Small clay figurines were probably used both in temple ceremonies and in people's homes. Among the best examples excavated to date at Petra are a group of three seated musicians and the representation of the Egyptian goddess Isis (equivalent to the Nabataean goddess Al 'Uzza and the Roman Aphrodite).

Petra is best known for its large, carved tomb facades funerary monuments to the kings but it also comprises a full urban infrastructure of temples, baths, houses, high places and cultic installations, niches, theatres, and elaborate water systems of pipelines, drainage networks, reservoirs and cisterns. Its entrance, through a 1.2-kilometre-long fissure through towering cliffs, is as dramatic as it was functional in assuring the defence of the city.

The legions of the Roman General Pompey swept into the area in 63 BC, and first controlled the region of the Decapolis (the "ten cities") in north Jordan and south Syria. For many centuries, Greco-Roman culture redrew the map of Jordan and the east Mediterranean, which were integrated into the south-eastern provinces of the Roman Empire. The stability and regional security that came with the pax Romana revitalised the international trade routes. The wealth from trade and from Roman political control fuelled an impressive urban boom whose legacy survives today in the impressive Roman towns of Gerasa (Jerash), Philadelphia (Amman), Gadara (Umm Qais), Abila (Qweilbeh) and Pella (Tabaqet Fahl). Not far from these major cities are scores of forts and provincial towns that comprised the agricultural and security hinterland of the frontier province — imposing legionary fortresses on the edge of the desert (Lejjun, Qasr el-Beshir, Udruh), isolated lookout towers (Zaafaran, Majra), and sprawling provincial cities that were not as grand as Gerasa and Philadelphia, but which indicate how the ordinary folk of the land lived off a variety of trading, agricultural and livestocking activities (Umm el-Jimal, Khirbet es-Samra, Umm el-Walid).

Recognising the strategic and commercial importance of the ancient route of the King's Highway, the Emperor Trajan ordered it rebuilt in the early 2nd Century AD as a veritable ancient two-lane paved highway that could carry Roman troops and supplies swiftly. Stretches of the road can still be seen in some parts of the country, especially near Umm el-Jimal and Khirbet es-Samra.

The overlay of Roman imperial culture on an ancient and strong foundation of indigenous Arabian/Semitic culture produced an impressive synthesis of art and culture that is testimony to the resilience of both peoples. Roman town plans, with neatly laid out streets and plazas, baths and markets became the urban rule — but with the habit of siting temples on hills and high places, following the local Semitic tradition. The gods of Rome and Northern Arabia were often fused into single deities. A common goddess was Tyche of

Antioch, who was the city goddess of Philadelphia (Amman). Classical artistic traditions quickly dominated the sculptors and artists of Roman Jordan. Stone busts were often used to mark the graves of the dead, while smaller figurines represented mythological figures such as Pan and a Centaur, or the goddess Aphrodite. Greek became the official language of public life. Most villagers, however, spoke and wrote the local Aramaic language, and many continued to worship their traditional Semitic or North Arabian gods.

The best preserved Roman period urban remains are at Jerash, half an hour by car north of Amman. Jerash was inhabited virtually without interruption for over one thousand years during the Hellenistic, Nabataean/Roman, Byzantine and early Islamic (Umayyad and Abbasid) periods, from the 2nd Century BC to the 9th Century AD. The earliest indigenous Arab/Semitic people in the 1st Millennium BC called their town Garshu. The Hellnistic settlement founded in the 2nd Century BC was called Antioch on the Chrysorhoas (or Antioch on the "Golden River", the name of the little river which still runs through the city). The Romans quickly Hellenised the former Arabic name Garshu into Gerasa. At the end of the 19th Century, the local Arab and Circassian inhabitants Arabised Roman "Gerasa" into today's Arabic name "Jerash".

The formal proclamation of the Byzantine Empire in 324 AD ushered in three centuries of relative continuity in the daily cultural habits and language of the local people, but with radical changes in religious practices and art. This is visible today in the many Byzantine churches that were built throughout the country, especially at Madaba, Mount Nebo, Jerash, Umm er-Resas, Rihab and Amman. The great artistic legacy of the Byzantine period in Jordan is the stunning collection of church floor mosaics, which reached their height of artistry in the 5th and 6th Centuries AD. The widespread proliferation of churches, and their mosaic representations of animals, people and pastoral scenes suggest that Byzantine Jordan was prosperous, pious and heavily populated, with an economy based heavily on agriculture, livestocking and agro-industries. As indicated by inscriptions on gravestones and other objects, the land continued to be a meeting place of different cultural and linguistic traditions from the greater Middle East region. Along with Greek, Aramaic and Arabic, the people of Jordan used the Syriac (Christo-Palestinian) script, and the Safaitic script of a largely nomadic people who ranged throughout Syria and Jordan from nearly 1,000 years, from the Hellenistic through the Byzantine periods.

In the 7th Century AD, the people and land of Jordan once again absorbed another major religious/political wave from beyond their territory the new power of Islam, which emerged from the Arabian Peninsula to the south in the early 7th Century AD and established the Umayyad dynasty in Damascus in 661 AD. Jordan suddenly found itself close to the regional centre of political power, and on a direct communications line between Damascus and the holy cities of Mecca and Medina, in the Islamic heartland of the Hijaz in western Saudi Arabia. Arabic became the predominant language and Islam the religion of the land, though an active Christian community with splendid churches always existed in Jordan, in keeping with Islam's tradition of tolerance and cultural pluralism.

Trade and agriculture were the main economic foundations of a population expansion which saw the expansion of Byzantine settlements, and greater exploitation of the desert fringe to the east thanks to sophisticed water management techniques reminiscent of the efficacy of Nabataean hydrology. The early Islamic "desert castles" east of Amman notably Amra, Kharana, and Hallabat are actually agricultural estates, baths, caravanseri and large residences. They were situated on important caravan routes that linked Damascus, the Amman-Azraq region, and the Arabian Peninsula. In south Jordan, in the 7th and 8th centuries, the port of Aqaba traded with China and North Africa.

Many Byzantine cultural traditions continued into the early Islamic years, as seen in works of art such as a bronze and iron brazier from Fedein (Mafraq) a particularly beautiful piece of work whose depictions of people, mythological birds and decorated niches brings together a complex legacy of art from Iran and the Greco-Roman Middle East. Like the fresco paintings of Qasr Amra or the architecture of Kharana, it clearly shows the synthesis of several regional artistic traditions. After nearly a century, these different traditions would be refined into a new identity that would come to be known as early Islamic art.

During the Abbasid, Fatimid and Ayyubid-Mamluke eras —spanning the nearly eight centuries after 750 AD the land of Jordan was more distant from the power centres of Baghdad and Cairo. Settlement patterns shifted towards a more subsistence lifestyle of small villages and farmsteads, whose more modest prosperity was reflected in cultural remains that were more functional and often less refinely decorated. After the disruptions of the Crusader period, which lasted about 100 years in Jordan and left behind two imposing castles at Kerak and Shobak, the Ayyubid-Mamluke era was a time of economic and political revival. The sugarcane industry flourished in the Jordan Valley, security was re-established, and prosperity derived largely from regional trade. With the defeat of the Mamlukes, Jordan found itself under the jurisdiction of the Ottoman Empire in the early 16th century, and maintained that status for four centuries, until the defeat of the Ottomans in 1918 and the birth of the modern state in the early 1920s.

Rami G. Khouri

8

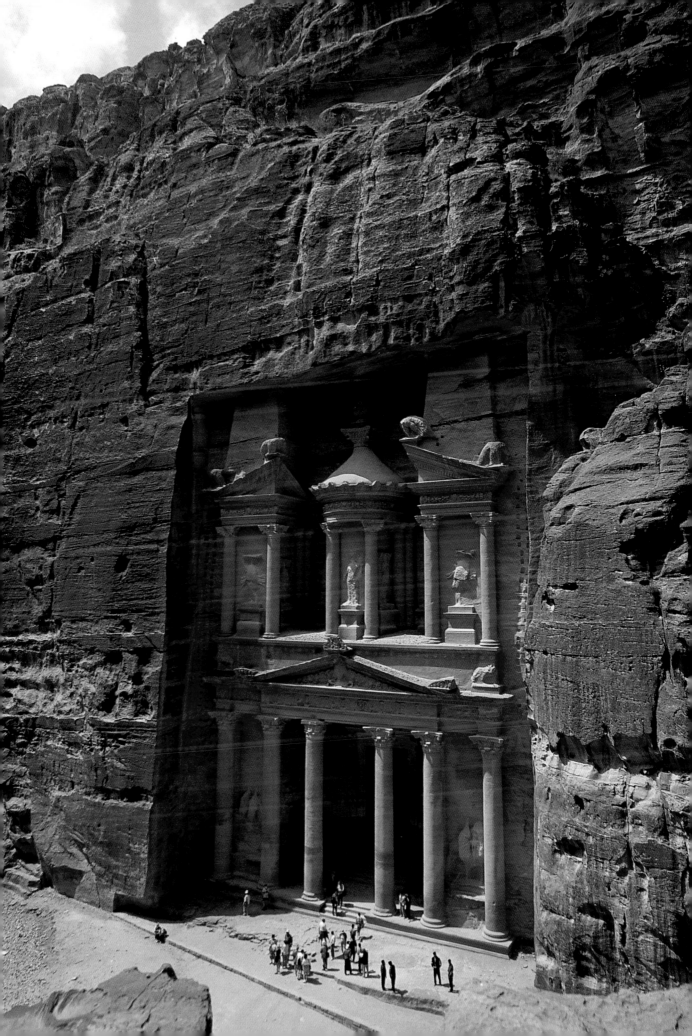

CRAFTS

The crafts of Jordan reflect fully the traditions which are more generally widespread in the Muslim world. They range from the production of carpets and kilim, still knotted or woven by hand on traditional looms, to objects in metal inlaid with scenes or in wood with mother-of-pearl insets, from weapons and jewellery of bedouin make to the pottery which still uses shapes and decorations dating back to the Middle Ages, from blown glass to textiles with fine cross-stitch embroidery. The town of Madaba, a particularly popular tourist site, is also famous for its carpets; both the classic handwoven and knotted carpets with geometric motives, as well as the charming kilim, decorated with naif designs which draw inspiration from the nomad life of the bedouins, can be found here. In recent years workshops have appeared in the capital where carpets and kilim still produced in the craft tradition use motives that have been reworked in a decidedly modern key. This production is highly interesting and original and, for those who appreciate it, fully merits the slightly higher cost. The same holds for Amman where the multitude of bazaars full of inexpensive souvenirs, frequently of rather unexceptional make, are flanked by shops that sell slightly more expensive, but choice wares, some of them produced many decades ago. The most interesting objects include belt daggers, their handles decorated with

These photos show some aspects of the Jordan crafts, which range from the production of carpets and kilim to objects in leather, or metal, from jewellery of bedouin make to embroidered textiles, pottery and blown glass.

scenes and with slightly curved blades, old rifles, cushions embroidered in tiny stitches with carefully chosen colours which form particularly striking and complex geometric patterns, as well as the silver bedouin jewellery. These ornaments, often enhanced by green or reddish agate, or simply glass paste inlays, are characterized by a rather rudimentary workmanship which however maintains intact the charm of the ornaments made several thousand years ago in the Mediterranean area, and where the forms and symbols are frequently reproposed, intermingled with other more recent motives of Islamic derivation. Articles of this sort, together with objects in leather related to a nomad way of life and the furnishings of the bedouin tents, can also be found fairly easily in Aqaba, while small bottles patiently filled with coloured sand are typical of Petra. Spices are a really good buy, for they are of excellent quality and low cost.

Views of Amman from the Citadel.

AMMAN

Clustered like a town in a Christmas manger scene around its splendid Roman theatre, the capital of Jordan has succeeded in merging what is left of its pluri-millenarian history with the demands of modern city life. On the site of the Biblical Rabbath Ammon, mentioned in Genesis, the city flourished under the Romans and was later endowed with a few interesting monuments in the early centuries of Islamic rule. Today, this city of a million inhabitants, a great metropolis that was only a modest town a hundred years ago, has preserved a residential urban fabric of relatively low buildings, fairly uniform in type and color, while modern skyscrapers house large hotels, banks, offices and shopping centres. In the newer zones, broad streets connect the various districts, named after the hill (jebel) where they are located, while the lower city, which was once the centre of the Roman Philadelphia, still has various picturesque streets where the lively market shops are to be found.

13

The remains of the colonnade of the Forum and a general view of the Roman Theatre in the city centre.

Four views of the Theatre with the well-preserved tiers.

THE LOWER CITY

The area of the **Theatre**, with the remains of the colonnade of the **Forum** and the gardens before it, is still the heart of the capital of Jordan. Full of life at all hours of the day, this zone is particularly crowded at dusk and on summer evenings. It is dominated by the imposing mass of the theatre, built between AD 169 and 177 and exploiting the natural slope, today picturesquely set within the dense urban fabric of the hill against which it stands. The theatre, with its three orders of seating tiers and a capacity of 6000 spectators, is well preserved, thanks also to restoration work which has permitted its use in various cultural events. The dazzling white structure has retained many of the decorative elements of the stage and of the orchestra; the vaulted corridors at the base of the theatre which served as entrance ways for the spectators have been rebuilt and now house two small museums that tourists to the area never fail to see. Northeast of the theatre, the stage wall aligned with the east side of the Forum, is the **Odeum**, a small covered theatre dating to the 2nd century AD. The orchestra area and the stage structure are well-preserved, while the tiers of seats, which had partially disappeared, have recently been rebuilt and can now once more, as formerly, accommodate 500 persons, and can be used for concerts and other events.

Traditional costumes from various bedouin tribes; on the right: a typical part of women's attire is the facial covering called "burgo", a variation of the veil, which offers protection from the sun.

MUSEUM OF JEWELLERY AND COSTUME

The **Museum of Jewellery and Costume**, also known as the **Museum of Folk Traditions**, is inside the original righthand entrance to the theatre. It offers an interesting panorama of the types of attire worn by men and women up to a few decades ago in the various regions of the country, a variety of headgear and veils for covering the women's faces, jewellery of bedouin manufacture as well as mosaics from various places.

The clothing, subdivided according to region, is richly embroidered in coloured cotton, while buttons and coins are often sewn onto the headgear and veils. Veils of this sort, which are almost like masks and leave only the eyes visible, are still in use in some of the bedouin communities as are the various types of jewellery beautifully exhibited in the showcases. These bracelets, anklets, pendant amulets and necklaces were made at the beginning of this century, and the techniques and styles clearly betray the influence of the traditional production of Syria, Egypt, Saudi Arabia and Yemen. Jewellery of this sort has gradually been replaced, above all in the more important centers, by commercially made gold

On the left, corsets and hats from Jerusalem, Bethlehem and Hebron. Above, two mosaics found in the Church of Elijah, Mary and Soreg in Jerash (late 6th cent. AD), one depicting a bird in a cage, symbol, in Byzantine iconography, of the human body, the second a vintage scene with a man, wearing a Phrygian cap and holding two bunches of grapes. Right, fragments of mosaics, one depicting two baskets of fruit, the other from Madaba, with a running deer.

and silver jewellery, probably preferred because it is more highly finished.

Craft production, sometimes rather crude but always with a charm of its own, began to disappear at the end of the 1960s. The fact that the State has set up this museum is therefore particularly important, for it both preserves the memory of a tradition that was once extremely widespread and it induces the population to treasure what still remains.

A long narrow gallery, on a lower level than the rest of the museum, houses fragments of mosaics from the zone of Madaba, dating to the 5th and 6th centuries. Most of them are decorations consisting of stylized acanthus or grape tendrils, which frame animals, religious images or figures drawn from agricultural life, drawn in a lively popular style where at times traces of the refined late Hellenistic tradition can still be felt.

21

FOLKLORE MUSEUM

Situated on the other side of the theatre, also inside one of the entrance galleries partially rebuilt in the course of restorations, the **Folklore Museum** houses a rich collection of traditional utensils and costumes, shown in realistic settings and with animated life-size mannequins. Some of the most interesting scenes include the bedouin wedding procession, reconstructed with particular care and with a wealth of details, weaving on a hand loom, as well as the scene of women talking together inside a traditional dwelling. To be noted the splendid round baskets hung on the walls: made of braided straw in

Weaving on a hand loom and two women talking, seated in a typical room.

bright colours, they were not so much meant to contain the food as to cover it, protecting it from the sun, dust and insects. The authentic highpoint of the museum is however the reconstruction of a nomad goatskin tent, demonstrating the subdivision of the space into areas for men and for women which was typical of the old Arab dwellings. Sometimes there was a third sector in the larger tents, meant for the guests. Tents of this sort are still to be found scattered throughout Jordan, sometimes alone, sometimes in groups, bearing witness to the continuity of traditions, even though various concessions to progress have been made, as witnessed, for instance, by the presence of an off-road vehicle often parked not far away.

A camel with the characteristic baldachin.

Reconstruction of a bedouin tent, called "beit el-shaar" (house of hair), made of goat skins, which are waterproof for they expand when it rains.

23

Above and right, the Temple of Hercules; left, the remains of a Byzantine church.

CITADEL

A road that climbs up the hill set opposite the theatre brings us in only a few minutes to the area of the **Citadel**, from which a splendid panorama of Amman can be had. The site, originally the acropolis of the ancient city, still contains traces of the fortifications of Roman times, frequently rebuilt in later periods, a temple of the 2nd century AD dedicated to Hercules and the remains of a 6th-century Byzantine church. A Spanish archaeological mission has moreover brought to light various rooms of a spacious complex built in the first period of Arab domination.

The **Temple of Hercules** was erected in honour of the Emperor Marcus Aurelius (161-180) on a high terrace, once connected to the city below via a monumental flight of stairs of which no trace remains. The sacred building, which probably stood on the site of an earlier sanctuary, had four Corinthian columns on the facade, two of which are still standing, complete with the tripartite architrave on top.

Left, the Audience Hall and details of the arcading with niches. On this page the remains of the walls and the paved Roman road of Al-Qasr.

The extensive ruins of the early medieval complex recently excavated and known as **Al-Qasr** lie to the northwest of the temple. Erected probably between 720 and 750, in other words in the final decades of Umayyad rule in the Islamic world, the complex served as the urban residence of the governor and as an administrative centre. Particularly interesting is the so-called *Audience Hall*, a square walled-in area 25 meters per side, with spacious rooms at the four corners, also square, and a central space, Greek cross in plan, in which most of the decoration is to be found. This consisted above all of blind arcading and niches carved in bas-relief in the stone or stucco and accented by complex geometrical patterns or highly stylized plant motives. Thanks to the excavations, which so far have been carried out in one part of the area, a paved Roman road flanked by porticoes has also come to light.

Above, a fragment of a colossal statue at the entrance to the Museum; the Museum entrance and below, head of Tyche, goddess of Fortune (2nd cent. AD).

ARCHAEOLOGICAL MUSEUM

Before leaving the hill of the Citadel, a visit to the **Archaeological Museum of Jordan** is a must. Not far from the base of the temple of Hercules, the building houses finds ranging in date from the Neolithic period to the Ottoman empire.

Among the most interesting objects of the earliest phase are a few anthropomorphic statues (one of them is the oldest one known), pottery of various types, Egyptian scarabs and Assyrian seals. Of particular note is the tomb of Jericho (ca. 1850 BC) rebuilt inside the museum. The stela of Baluah (Balu'a), on which a Moabite king and two mid-Eastern divinities are shown, dates to the 12th century BC, while the haunting anthropoid terracotta sarcophagi were made three centuries later. They still have the handles to which the ropes were tied so they could be let down into the pit. The excavations in the area of the Citadel of Amman have yielded both the two-faced heads, probably used as capitals, and the famous statue of Yerahazar (Yerah 'Azar) in limestone. To be particularly noted in ad-

Left, above: finely executed head in stone; below, a terra cotta anthropoid sarcophagus from Jebel el-Qusour, dating to the second Iron Age (1000-539 BC); above, right, marble statue of Daedalus, copy of a Hellenistic original, found in Amman.

Left, stone statuette probably of a Nabataean priest; above, terra cotta figurines of Aphrodite, from Jawa, dated to the 2nd cent. AD; below, the famous two-faced heads (7th cent. BC) unearthed in the Citadel of Amman, and used as capitals.

Right, fragment of an architectural relief and an example of the rich and elegant Islamic decorative art.

dition to the numerous finds of Persian, Hellenistic and Nabataean art are various interesting pieces dating to Roman times, including a fine statue of Apollo, found in Sebastye, the head of a woman from Jerash, and the famous head of Tyche, goddess of fortune. Last but not least in the museum collections are the famous Dead Sea manuscripts, which mention a fabulous treasure in the texts, and a few finds from the Byzantine and Islamic periods.

Above, two views of the Mosque of Abu Darwish.

Below, The Housing Bank Center, one of the many buildings of the modern city.

Right, two pictures of the Mosque of Malik Abdallah.

THE MODERN CITY

Intelligent town planning, shifting the industrial settlements to the area northeast of Amman, has saved the city from this source of pollution, while the network of through-traffic routes means that only in the rush hour is traffic intense. The two **mosques of Abu Darwish** and **of Malik Abdallah** can be seen from many parts of the city. The former, set on the hill of al-Ashrafiya, is unique in its decoration in two-coloured stone; the latter is far more imposing, characterized by twin minarets and an enormous dome covered in blue majolica tiles. The building, which the capital takes great pride in, dates to the early 1990s and was designed by one of the best contemporary Jordanian architects. The people are also proud of the modern Sports City, Palace of Culture and Monument to the War Dead with the annexed Armed Forces Museum, as well as their numerous skyscrapers with offices, shopping centres, restaurants and other entertainment centres for adults and children.

33

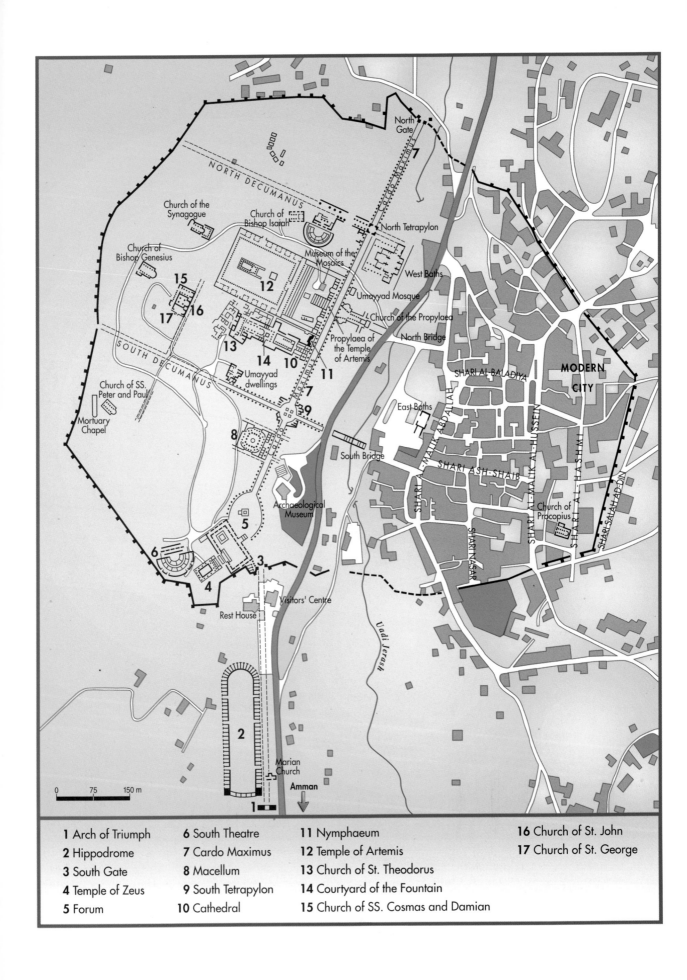

NORTH DECUMANUS

Church of the Synagogue

Church of Bishop Isaiah

North Gate

7

North Tetrapylon

Church of Bishop Genesius

Museum of the Mosaics

West Baths

15

16

17

12

Umayyad Mosque

Church of the Propylaea

13

14

10

Propylaea of the Temple of Artemis

North Bridge

SOUTH DECUMANUS

11

SHARI AL-BALADIYA

MODERN CITY

Church of SS. Peter and Paul

Umayyad dwellings

7

East Baths

Mortuary Chapel

3

9

8

South Bridge

SHARI ASH-SHAIB

SHARI AL-MALIK ABDALLAH

SHARI AL-MALIK AL-HUSSEIN

5

Archaeological Museum

SHARI NASAR

Church of Procopius

SHARI AL-HASHMI

SHARI SALAH AD-DIN

6

4

3

Visitors' Centre

Rest House

Wadi Jerash

2

Marian Church

Amman

0   75   150 m

1

1 Arch of Triumph	**6** South Theatre	**11** Nymphaeum	**16** Church of St. John
2 Hippodrome	**7** Cardo Maximus	**12** Temple of Artemis	**17** Church of St. George
3 South Gate	**8** Macellum	**13** Church of St. Theodorus	
4 Temple of Zeus	**9** South Tetrapylon	**14** Courtyard of the Fountain	
5 Forum	**10** Cathedral	**15** Church of SS. Cosmas and Damian	

The Arch of Triumph erected in honour of Hadrian.

JERASH

The formal town plan first laid down around 70 AD reflected the typical Roman scheme of a main colonnaded street intersected by smaller colonnaded side streets. When the Emperor Trajan occupied all of Jordan in 106 AD, Gerasa fell under the jurisdiction of the new Roman Province of Arabia. As local investments in agriculture, industry and services boosted regional and international trade, Jerash and all of Jordan enjoyed a golden age for over 200 years. A visitor senses Gerasa's prosperity even before reaching the modern entrance to the site through the ancient city's recently restored South Gate. The first monument one encounters on the road from Amman is the triple-gated Hadrian's Arch, standing along some 450 metres south of the city walls and built to commemorate the Emperor Hadrian's visit to Gerasa in 129 AD. The arch stands next to the massive Hippodrome, with its reconstructed south end.

The South Gate leads visitors into the spacious skewed Oval Plaza, with its long arcade of Ionic columns. Overlooking the plaza from the west is the 1st Century AD Temple of Zeus, whose Hellenistic predecessor has recently been uncovered in its lower courtyard. West of the temple is the large South Theatre, finished in the early 2nd Century AD and still sporting inscriptions with the names of its benefactors. The Oval Plaza leads into the 800-metre-long Cardo, the main street and urban spine of ancient Gerasa. In the 2nd Century AD, the original Cardo was widened and its original Ionic columns and capitals were replaced by the more elaborate Corinthian style (except for the

Oval Plaza and a stretch of the Cardo in the very north of the city).

The city's most important structures, arranged around the Cardo, included markets, temples, fountains and other buildings. Walking up the street today from south to north, the visitor passes a string of public monuments, some of which retain the crisp carved stonework of the 2nd Century AD: the Agora, or Forum, where official and commercial business was transacted; the South Tetrakionia intersection with the South Decumanus; the richly carved entrance to a Roman temple which was transformed into a church (the so-called Cathedral) in the Byzantine period; the Nymphaeum, or ornate public fountain, with its rich stonework still sporting remnants of ancient paintwork; the delicately carved and stately entrance to the monumental processional way up to the city's main cultic site, the Temple of Artemis (daughter of Zeus, sister of Apollo, and patron goddess of the city); the massive, unexcavated West Baths; the once domed North Tetrapyla forming the intersection with the North Decumanus; the small North Theatre, with inscriptions noting the seats of individual tribes in the city council; and the North Colonnaded Street leading to the North Gate.

In the Byzantine era, some of Gerasa's Roman temples were transformed into Christian churches, while new churches were built from cut stones and columns taken from Roman era buildings that had collapsed from frequent earthquakes in antiquity. We know of at least 15 churches in Byzantine Gerasa. The complex of three churches dedicated to

35

Above, the inner gate of the Arch of Triumph; below, the outer wall of the Hippodrome; right above, the South Gate and, in the photo below, the remains of the Temple of Zeus.

St George, St. John, and SS Cosmas and Damian, west of the Temple of Artemis, has the city's best preserved mosaics from the 6th Century AD, including representations of animals and the church benefactors and bishops.

Rami G. Khouri

VISIT TO THE EXCAVATIONS

About half a kilometre from the southern entrance to the city is the solitary Arch of Triumph, erected in AD 129 in honour of the visit of the Emperor Hadrian. This imposing construction with three openings is enriched by niches which once housed statues that have now disappeared. The ashlars in ochre-coloured stone used to build this splendid monument are enhanced by extremely fine decorative elements, above all in the mouldings which surround the niches and openings, at the springing of the arches, as well as in the lower part of the four half-columns which articulate the facade. Set on high pedestals, these half-columns seem to spring from elegant baskets of acanthus leaves, which must certainly have been echoed in the Corinthian capitals which once stood at the top.

After passing the Arch of Triumph, the path moves along the outer wall of the Hippodrome, built be-

The Forum, with, in the foreground, the oval piazza with the column topped by a metal frieze at the centre.

tween the 1st and 3rd century and once capable of containing as many as 5000 spectators. Recent excavations by a Polish mission in the ruins of the building have brought to light the remains of stables and two towers. Jordanian archaeologists have unearthed the remains of a small church dating to the 6th century on the opposite side of the road.

The Visitors Centre is located just outside the excavation area, and has an efficient information office as well as a large model of the Roman city which is particularly useful for orientation purposes.

The real entrance to the extensive area over which the ruins of ancient Gerasa are scattered is from the South Gate, built in the 1st century AD together with the other three gates which opened in the Roman walls, but which were surely remodelled

when the arch of triumph was erected, which served as inspiration for the acanthus leaf motives at the base of the half-columns which here too are set against the facade. Immediately to the left of the south gate is a spacious esplanade, dominated by a height on which the remains of the **Temple of Zeus** are to be found. Built in 162-163 BC, it stands on the site of an earlier Roman temple of the 1st century which had probably replaced an even older Greek temple, also dedicated to the highest pagan divinity. The view over the Forum below, with its unique elliptical shape, is particularly fine from the large piazza in front of the temple.

THE FORUM

The so-called oval piazza, (actually sort of horse-shoe shaped, a form that might indicate eastern in-

fluence), is surrounded by a colonnade that is still well preserved, with all of 56 Ionic columns still standing, surmounted by a tripartite architrave. Shops once faced out over the colonnade, which was probably a portico. The fact that the original paving, composed of limestone slabs which gradually get smaller as they move towards the center, still exists, makes this structure even more interesting and fascinating.

The foundations of a monument with a square base stand at the centre of the square. It was later transformed into a fountain and the channels which are still clearly visible in the paving housed tubes which brought water from a cistern located in the northern part of the city. A column on a square base was erected in the centre of the Forum in recent years, with a metal frieze on top inside which a symbolic flame is lit on those days when the annual International Festival is held in Jerash.

Four fascinating shots of the South Theatre.

THEATRE

Northwest of the height on which the Temple of Zeus rises is the wonderful structure of the **South Theatre**, so-called to distinguish it from the smaller theatre on the other side of the city which is not nearly as well preserved. Built during the reign of Domitian (81-96) to replace an older building, this theatre was carefully restored in 1953, both as a tourist attraction and so that it could be used in public events. The cavea, composed of two orders of tiers with 32 rows of seats in all, can accommodate 3000 spectators. The orchestra and the scena, set on a podium with twelve niches, are also in excellent condition. The presence of the podium made it possible to use the orchestra space as a large pool, thanks to waterproof partitions which were inserted into the grooves that are still visible at the sides of the two entrances. The architectural structures of the lower tier of the stage wall, sumptuously decorated with colonnades, niches and monumental gates, are still almost intact.

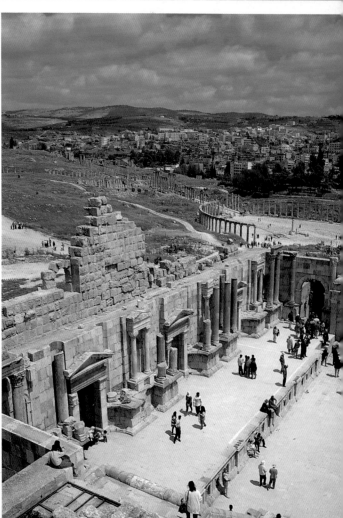

The Cardo Maximus flanked by columns; left, detail of the colonnade.

CARDO MAXIMUS

The ruins of Gerasa (Jerash) are even more spectacular thanks to the broad paved street which begins at the north side of the Forum and continues for about 800 meters to the North Gate. This is the **Cardo Maximus**, the main artery of the city, once flanked by porticoes of which over 500 columns still exist, many of which still have their capitals. Originally Ionic in style and dating to the first century AD it was rebuilt in Corinthian style a century later. The intersection points with the two decumani were marked by four-sided arches.

Moving north along the cardo maximus, the ruins of the **Macellum** appear on the left, with many of the columns still standing on their original bases, although the upper part of the

shaft has been lost. The next stop is the round piazza which marks the intersection with the south decumanus, with the four pilasters with niches which constituted the base of the monumental **South Tetrapylon** standing in the centre.

Not much further on, once more on the left, two other interesting buildings are to be found. The first was the ancient **Cathedral** of the city, built in the second half of the 4th century on the area and with materials taken from the temple of Dionysus. All that remains is the richly decorated portal and a few traces of the ground plan of this three-aisled basilica. The second, right next to it, is in a better state of preservation. This is the **Nymphaeum**, a monumental fountain dating to the late 2nd century AD; the concave wall subdivided into two tiers of niches is still standing up to the springing of the semi-dome which covered it, and which has disappeared as has most of the marble and painted stucco facing.

Left, above, the Macellum; below, the Southern Tetrapylon; at the side: the Cathedral and, below, the Nymphaeum.

Above, the Propylaea of the Temple of Artemis; right, the sacred enclosure surrounded by columns (details in the photo below).

Then come the **Propylaea** of the imposing **Temple of Artemis**, protecting divinity of the city. Built in various phases, the most important of which dates to the 2nd century AD, the temple is preceded by two staircases which lead to an external portico, which in turn leads into a rectangular temenos (sacred enclosure), measuring 161 by 120 metres. The actual cult building is set on a high podium: the elegant Corinthian columns set on the eastern side of the peristyle are still almost intact, while the marble facing of the cella, decorated with rectangular niches surmounted by pediments, has been lost. As was often the case with structures in the Syrian area, the temple is preceded by a sacrificial altar. In the Byzantine period and in the early centuries of Arab domination, potters' workshops were housed inside this imposing complex, still partially cluttered by the remains of subsequent constructions.

Right to the south of the Temple of Artemis, in the area behind the Cathedral, stand the ruins of the **Church of Saint Theodorus** and the so-called **Court of the Fountain**. The former, built as a basilica with three aisles at the end of the 5th century, preserves interesting remains of mosaics. The latter, set between the apse of the church of Saint Theodorus and the Cathedral, orginally served as atrium for the church. The square basin inside was used annually to commemorate the miracle of the wedding of Cana. Continuing along the cardo maximus beyond the Temple of Artemis and turning left at the crossing with the northern decumanus, we arrive at the ruins of the **North Theatre**, built around AD 165 and used as odeum until the 5th-6th century.

Left, the Church of St. Theodorus and the Court of the Fountain; below, the North Theatre.

Remains of Byzantine churches. Above, the floor mosaic of the Church of SS. Cosmas and Damian; below, what remains of the churches of St. John and St. George.

Before leaving the ruins of Jerash it is worth while to take a look at the remains of a group of Byzantine churches built around 533, under the reign of Justinian. The most interesting is the **Church of SS. Cosmas and Damian**, of which most of the mosaic floor still exists. In the part which was once the nave, the floor has a complex decoration of a geometric layout with square elements with a light-coloured background in which various symbolic, above all zoomorphic, figures are to be found. On the site of the choir a dedicatory inscription is flanked by the portraits of the patrons, Theodorus and Georgia. Right next to it, also in the area south-west of the Temple of Artemis, the vestiges of two other Byzantine churches can be seen. The first, consecrated to **St. John**, contains mosaics which depict, among other things, various Egyptian cities. The second, dedicated to **St. George**, and in basilical plan, continued to be used for worship up to the 8th century.

Above, view of the zone of Ajlun; right, the Castle of Qalat ar-Rabad and, in the photo below, three pictures of interiors.

AJLUN

The place is famous for its imposing castle, known as **Qalat ar- Rabad**, which dominates the landscape from a few kilometres away. It is one of the best preserved medieval fortified structures in Jordan, and from its height of 1250 metres it furnishes spectacular views over the valley of the Jordan.

Built by the Arabs of the Ayyubid dynasty around 1185, conquered and destroyed by the Mongols in 1260, the fortress was immediately rebuilt and enlarged by the Mamluke sultan Baibars. The castle was once surrounded by a broad moat with a drawbridge, now replaced by a board walk. After a series of U-bend entrances and various gateways sometimes set into the towers, a steep ramp leads to the upper redoubt. The best view is to be had from here. Some of the most interesting rooms include casemates with arrowslits and rooms covered with cross or barrel vaulting.

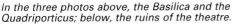

In the three photos above, the Basilica and the Quadriporticus; below, the ruins of the theatre.

Left, the Lake of Tiberias.

UMM QAYS

Founded around the end of the 4th century BC, the ancient Gadara was from the beginning a prestigious cultural centre and was the birthplace of the Greek philosophers Menippus and Philodemus, as well as the poet Meleager. Its fame continued intact under Augustus, but as a result of its political leanings, it was semi-destroyed by the Romans in the year 70. The area of the excavations, rather extensive, includes the ruins of a large **Basilica**, a **Quadriporticus**, a bath and two theatres, the largest of which, on the north, still has most of its tiers and seats in basalt with back-rests once reserved for the authorities. Of particular interest are the numerous Greco-Roman tombs (of the Germani, of Modestus, of Chaireas), the subterranean mausoleum of Roman date, and the colonnaded street that connected the area of the north theatre to the monumental gate about a kilometre and a half to the west. Important remains of the shops that lined this long artery are still to be found along the initial stretch. An Ottoman village was built with reused material on the area where the acropolis was once located. Two recently restored buildings contain the archaeological museum and the Rest House, from the terrace of which there is a splendid view over the heights of the Golan, the Lake of Tiberias and the Valley of the Jordan.

THE VALLEY OF THE JORDAN

A river packed with symbolic meaning and historical memories, the source of the Jordan lies in Mount Hermon. After a winding journey of 330 kilometres which crosses the Lake of Tiberias it flows into the Dead Sea. Thanks to various recent hydrological works, an intensive agriculture has been introduced into this valley, which was already fertile, notably increasing the production of fruit and vegetables.

Two pictures of the Valley of the Jordan.

The excavations of Pella.

PELLA

Gradually brought back to light in the course of recent excavations, the ruins of Pella are scattered throughout a particularly fascinating area which was already settled in prehistoric times, as witnessed by numerous finds. Of the Hellenistic city, which subsequently became part of the Roman empire, the remains of a small 1st century AD theatre and various churches have been brought to light, including a three-aisled basilica with Corinthian columns and a mosaic floor.

Qasr al-Hallabat: one of the entrances to the castle.

On the following page: detail of a portal; an arch and a corner tower built in blocks of light-coloured limestone with dark bands of basalt.

THE DESERT CASTLES

Built or at least remodeled for new uses in the first half of the 8th century, just when the Umayyad dynasty,.after reaching the zenith of its power, was beginning to acquire a decorative symbolical idiom and a formal attention to the court ceremonial which had initially been absent in the Muslim world, the so-called castles of the desert were residential complexes located outside the urban areas, meant to be used every so often by the caliph and his entourage. Spread here and there in Syrian and Jordanian soil (but there are also others in the territory at present occupied by Israel), many of these castles are to be found in the surroundings of Amman, although at the time the capital of the Islamic world was Damascus. The concept of "desert castle" is actually fairly recent and a result of the fact that many of these complexes are in areas that are now denuded, and often difficult to reach without an off-road vehicle, but when they were built they stood in the midst of a well-irrigated territory, with a luxuriant vegetation.

QASR AL-HALLABAT

Distinguished by its building material - blocks of light-coloured limestone and dark basalt from the volcanic region of the Hauran - this castle was rebuilt by the Umayyads on a site that was originally occupied by a Nabataean outpost, followed by a Roman fortress, and finally a Byzantine monastery. Nothing but portions of ruined walls and piles of stone remain today of this square structure with corner towers. A few extant architectural elements which have miraculously survived (such as the polylobate arch flanked by columns on one of the entrances) provide an idea of its original elegance. Further confirmation of the attention paid to the aesthetic aspect rather than to the defensive functions is shown by the presence in almost all the rooms of mosaic floors, now covered by a thin layer of earth to ensure their preservation.

Qasr al-Azraq. Above, the entrance; right, the mosque and below, a view of the inside.

QASR AL-AZRAQ

Probably built by the Romans at the end of the 3rd century, this castle then passed into the hands of the Umayyads, but was completey rebuilt in 1236-37, under the Ayyubid dynasty, as indicated by the inscription set on the main entrance. The castle however owes its fame above all to the fact that the legendary Lawrence of Arabia sojourned here in the winter of 1917, charged by the English secret services to incite the Arabs to revolt against the Ottoman empire, and it was from this fortress that he organized the battle of Aqaba.

Of interest, in the entrance vestibule, is the collection of plaques with inscriptions in Latin and Greek or bas-reliefs of plant or animal motives. To be noted too are the heavy monolithic doors in basalt, some of which are still in place in the building. The mosque in the courtyard dates to the Ayyubid period. It stands in an oblique position so that the orientation towards Mecca of the back wall could be respected.

Qasr or Qusayr Amra: the exterior and a frescoed vault in the Audience Hall.

Right, above: the dome of the bath with frescoes of the signs of the zodiac; below, a detail of the frescoes in the Audience Hall.

QASR or QUSAYR AMRA

Fundamental for an understanding of the characterists of Islamic art in its formative phase, this building was probably built as a place where the Umayyad caliph al-Walid I (705-715) could find restoration and diversion.This same caliph was also responsible for the spectacular Great Mosque of Damascus. The name of Qusayr (small castle) with which this building is better known is due to its small size, fully compensated for by the profusion of decoration, which lends it a distinctive character all its own. The walls of the building - which in the surviving portion is constituted essentially of an audience hall with three aisles covered with barrel vaults and a bath (hamman) inspired by the Roman baths - are in fact completely covered with frescoes, probably by Syrian or Arabian artists. The pictures,

packed with symbolism which celebrates the power of the caliph, are however not always leggible: on the wall to the right of the entrance, for example, the rulers of the earth who are paying homage to the Muslim sovereign can barely be made out. The hunting scenes and the decorations of the bath are better preserved. Particularly of note is a cupola frescoed with astrological figures.

Qasr al-Kharana. The imposing mass of the castle, the courtyard and an inner room decorated with stuccoes.

QASR AL-KHARANA

The splendid state of preservation and imposing aspect more than justify the name of castle for **Qasr al-Kharana** which rises up from a bare plain about 60 km. southeast of Amman. Completely rebuilt or at least remodelled by the Umayyads in 711, the building stands on the site of preceding Roman and then Byzantine structures, probably rebuilt in the 7th century when the area was briefly conquered by the Sassanian Persians. The semicircular towers and narrow arrowslits which articulate the facades of this massive square building have led many scholars to believe that it had a real defensive function, which however seems to be contradicted by the fact that many of the arrowslits do not correspond with the level of the floors, and could therefore not have been used. The painstaking stucco decoration inside also seems to indicate that the building was meant to be a typically sumptuous residence for the caliph.

QASR AL-MUSHATTA

This extraordinary complex, which rises from the desert not far from the airport of Amman, might have been one of the most interesting of the castles of Umayyad times thanks to the extraordinary refinement of its decorations, carved in bas-relief in a porous rosy-hued limestone. Unfortunately, however, almost the entire frieze which decorated the facade has been removed and is now on exhibit in the Islamic Museum in Berlin. Nevertheless the few decorative elements still in situ succeed in giving us an idea of the high quality of the work, a fusion of the finest Greco-Roman tradition with elements of Persian derivation.

Building, begun by Caliph al-Walid II in 743, was interrupted at his death and remained incomplete. What remains today includes stretches of the fortified enclosure, a square of 148 metres per side, and the vestiges of an elaborate entrance vestibule and the throne room behind it.

UMM AL-JIMAL

An outing to Umm al-Jimal, a haunting centre abandoned for centuries and almost entirely built of the dark basalt typical of the area of Jebel Druso, is not perhaps really a part of the itinerary of visits to the desert castles, for it is somewhat more to the north. The city, founded by the Nabataeans in the 1st century BC and which then passed to the Romans, the Ghassanids (Christian Arabs) and the Byzantines before becoming part of the Islamic world, for centuries had achieved considerable prosperity, as the name, which in Arab means "the mother of camels" seems to indicate. Around the end of the 8th century it was half destroyed by an earthquake and abandoned. The ruins occupy a vast area, partially enclosed in the circle of walls. Mostly churches and other public buildings, from a distance they look like disorderly piles of ruins, but up close reveal traces of the mind that produced them (of interest the building techniques of the roofs), as well as various aspects of the daily life that once went on here.

Qasr al-Mushatta and, on the right, the ruins of the city of Umm al-Jimal.

MADABA

A city of ancient origins, cited in the Bible as Medba, Madaba was attacked and destroyed around the 10th century B.C. by the Aramaeans and the Ammonites but was rebuilt shortly thereafter. The height of its splendor probably coincides with the early centuries of the Christian era, when, under Byzantine dominion, it became the centre of a flourishing school of mosaic workers. And still today the mosaics - found from the late nineteenth century on in the floors of churches, dwellings and shops - constitute the principal attraction of the city, next to remains of Roman times that an Italo-American mission is attempting to bring back to light. The first to be discovered and still the most famous is the floor mosaic of the **Greek-Orthodox church of St. George**, dating to the times of Justinian, where a sort of **geographic map of Palestine** is depicted, for the benefit of the pilgrims on their way to the Holy Land. To be recognized in the surviving fragments are the cities of Jerusalem, Bethlehem and Jerico, as well as the river Jordan, the Lake of Tiberias and the Dead Sea.

The Greek Orthodox church of St. George in which the mosaic with the plan of Palestine is to be found.

Right, a detail of the mosaic showing the city of Jerusalem.

67

Archaeological and Folklore Museum: fragments of mosaic floors and objects in pottery found in the zone of Madaba.

Madaba also has an interesting **Archaeological and Folklore Museum** to offer to its visitors, in which the exhibits include fragments of mosaic floors found inside buildings that no longer exist, architectural elements and jewellery and pottery from Roman and Byzantine times, Hellenistic, Nabataean, Roman, Byzantine and Arab coins, in addition to Assyrian seals and Egyptian scarabs.

The **Cathedral**, 200 metres from the Church of St. George, also merits a visit. The fine floor is dated to the year 562 with hunting and pastoral scenes, fish and birds, inserted into a striking geometric composition. Then there is also the **Church of the SS. Apostles**, built in 578 on the south slope of the hill, and we

Church of the SS. Apostles. Left above, mosaic with the female personification of the ocean. Below and above right, details of the mosaics.

The Church of SS. Lot and Procopius in Khirbet al-Mukhayyat: floor mosaic.

even know the name of the artist-a certain Salamanios-who made the magnificent mosaic floor, characterized by tesserae of particularly bright colours. The design is organized around a large central medallion depicting a woman who personifies the sea, emerging from the center of a geometric decoration that consists of an allover pattern of facing pairs of birds separated by a plant motive. Another band, with acanthus volutes containing human figures, completes the decoration.

The village of **Khirbet al-Mukhayyat**, on the road leading to Mount Nebo, contains another mosaic found in an excellent condition in 1935 inside the **Church of SS. Lot and Procopius**: included in the design are two panels with vine tendrils framing scenes of hunting, vintage, and dance.

Above, left, Mount Nebo overlooking the valley of Jordan. In the other photos, the church and monastery complex.

MOUNT NEBO

The enormous symbolic significance of this site, bound both to the Jewish and Christian religious traditions, explains why it exerts such fascination. Situated ten or so kilometres from Madaba at an altitude of about 800 metres, the view from here sweeps over the entire valley of the Jordan as far as the Dead Sea. For, according to the Bible, this is the very mountain Yahveh told Moses to climb so that he could see the promised land before dying, and it is here that Moses was then buried. A cross signs the spot chosen to commemorate his death. On the presumed site of his tomb a monastery was built, and since 1933 the ruins are gradually being brought to light by the Holy Land Franciscans, who are still at work studying and restoring. In this area, called Jebel (mount) Siyagha from the Aramaic siyagha which means "monastery", in addition to the vestiges of a small church, described as early as the 4th century by a Roman pilgrim, the remains of a religious building of Byzantine times, dating to various moments in the 6th century, are to be found. This building, of which nothing now remains but the base, has been covered by a stable structure in masonry.

Once a large three-aisled basilica, there was a baptistery and a room (known as diaconicon) used by the deacons for the preparation of the consecrated vessels. This room, raised by about a metre in the 6th century, is where the sumptuous mosaic floor below was discovered in the summer of 1976. Finished in 531 and signed by the mosaic craftsmen Soelos, Kaiomos and Elijah, hunting and pastoral scenes are set in four superposed registers, with a long inscription at the top, enclosed in a plait. The lower register is unique, with two men (one of whom is black) holding an ostrich, a zebra and a dromedary on leashes.

The Chapel of the Virgin (in Greek Theotokos, Mother of God), located in the southern part of the church, dates to the first decade of the 7th century; the floor mosaic was comprised of a rectangular panel, with gazelles separated by plant motives and two bulls flanking an altar, illustrating a psalm in the Bible, the text of which ("Then they will offer bulls on your altar") is set above the panel.

The present covered structure, preserves, in addition to mosaics and architectureal elements from the

On this page: mosaic fragments found inside the church. Right, the large floor mosaic with hunting and pastoral scenes. Below, a view of the inside of the church.

church (such as the lower parts of some of the columns and capitals carved in bas-relief), fragments of mosaics from other buildings in the area. Set vertically to differentiate them from the original floor mosaics of the basilica, they belong to different periods. Some of them even date to the late 7th and 8th centuries, in other words the period in which the area had already fallen into Muslim hands, as witnessed by the inscriptions in Arab, as well as Greek, set next to some of the decorations.

DEAD SEA

In the Crusader period the Europeans dubbed this great salt lake, covering an area of 920 sq. km., the Dead Sea. About 50 km. from Amman, it lies at the bottom of a natural depression that reaches 394 metres below sea level. The waters, rich in mineral salts, contain four times the amount of sodium chloride as is found normally in ocean water, making it unsuitable for plant and animal life, but ideal for spas and medical treatments. Establishments specialized in treating skin diseases are springing up on its banks. Two of the most modern are situated on the northern shore of the Dead Sea, near the village of Suwayma. But the one of **Hammamat Main** is particularly charming, located further to the southeast, almost at the mouth of the Wadi Zerqa Main, in natural surroundings of particular beauty thanks to picturesque waterfalls. The therapeutic properties of these waters were already known and exploited in antiquity.

Right, the cascades of Hammamat Main.

The typical formations of mineral salts in the Dead Sea.

What remains of Umm ar-Rasas.

UMM AR-RASAS

Among the latest archaeological discoveries of the early medieval period are the ruins of Umm ar-Rasas. Nabataean in origin, the site then passed to the Romans and Byzantines before becoming part of the Islamic territory. A complex of four churches has been brought to light in the settlement, which still retains the rectangular enclosing walls erected by the Byzantines. A magnificent floor mosaic that was practically intact was brought to light in 1986 in one of these churches, dedicated to **St. Stephen**. The complex decoration is composed of a central rectangular panel with scrolling grapevine tendrils surrounded by a figured frame of particularly intense colours. The two longitudinal strips which separated the nave area from the aisles contain sixteen vignettes of the towns in Palestine and Transjordan, beginning with Jerusalem. Twelve other vignettes of towns in the Egyptian Delta, including Alexandria, are to be found in various sections of the floor, together with inscriptions, portraits of the patrons, as well as hunting, pastoral and harvesting scenes

On this page: above, the magnificent floor mosaic of the Church of St. Stephen; below, two details of the mosaic with the ancient cities of Neapolis and Philadelphia.

Three details of the mosaics of the Church of St. Stephen. Left: the ancient city of Sebastye; above and below: plant motives.

Further details of the floor mosaic found in St. Stephen with figures of plants and animals. In the photo below, fishing scenes in the outer frame.

Left, view of the two sides of the Wadi Mujib.

Above, two pictures of the Temple of Ar-Rabba: in the foreground, a fine column with a Corinthian capital.

WADI MUJIB

A course of water, called Arnon in antiquity, marked the border between the lands of two peoples mentioned in the Bible, the Amorrites and the Moabites, settled respectively to the north and south. This course of water, today known as **Wadi Mujib**, empties into the Dead Sea after running though a spectacular ravine, near which is the line of the ancient Roman road. This was one of the arteries built by Trajan after he annexed the Nabataean kingdom, in AD 106. To be seen in the area are also the remains of a bridge, a fortified building and other structures dating to Nabataean, Byzantine and Arab times. About twenty kilometres further south stands al-Qasr, an Arab village built of architectural elements from a 2nd-century AD Nabataean temple.

Another 5 km. further south is **Ar-Rabba**, a small centre that rose on the ruins of a fortress mentioned in the Bible, and which then passed into the hands of the Nabataeans, the Romans and the Byzantines. Remains of the Roman city, called Areopolis, include a well-preserved temple, inside which dedications to Diocletian and Maximianus can still be read, and various Corinthian columns which were part of a colonnaded road.

AL-KERAK

The locality of al-Kerak, now the site of a flourishing inhabited center, is known for the imposing **fort** erected in the first half of the 12th century by the Crusaders and which was then taken over by the Arabs, who consolidated and enlarged the building in 1263. This spectacular fortress is located at an altitude of about 1000 m., in a dominating position where the ancient capital of the Moabite kingdom, also cited in the Bible, had once stood, to become, after centuries of decadence, the seat of an import bishopric in Byzantine times.

The north side of the castle, which is trapezoid in shape and surrounded by a moat most of which is now filled in, is particularly imposing with its two towers that project from the massive walls, which have no other openings but the narrow arrowslits. The east side, which overlooks the valley of the Ay as-Sitt, is also almost all the work of the Crusaders. Here four rectangular towers are connected to the curtain walls. Restoration work on the south side was however done by the Arabs, where a cistern for water in case of siege was built, as well as many of the constructions which close the lower courtyard to the west, including the buttresses of the outermost circle. The two construction phases can be distin-

guished thanks to the different materials used by the Crusaders and the Arabs: a dark hard volcanic stone by the former, a light soft carefully squared limestone by the latter. Particularly spectacular is the view from the top of the upper court of the castle, which embraces the Dead Sea and the valley of the Jordan. Some of the vaulted rooms can also be seen as well as rooms once used as an oil mill and as a bakery.

The lower courtyard consists of a spacious terrace with various rooms on the valley side. These house a small **Archaeological Museum**, which contains finds from the area dating to between the early Bronze Age and the early Middle Ages.

Three views of the exterior and interior of the Fort of al-Kerak; below, panorama from the top of the castle.

Qasr Ash-Shawbak. Pictures of the castle and of a well-preserved tower. Above, right, view of the inside and, below, the remains of the Crusader chapel.

QASR ASH-SHAWBAK

Although on the whole less well preserved than the preceding, the castle of Shawbak vaunts a setting that makes it perhaps even more fascinating, for unlike al-Kerak, now to all extents besieged by the buildings of the inhabited center, it is in a completely isolated position, overlooking a farflung panorama where no trace of modern times is to be seen.

The fortress, located about halfway between al-Kerak and Petra, along the famous "King's Highway", was built in 1115 by Baldwin, Frankish king of Jerusalem, to keep the route that connected Syria and Egypt under control, and it was initially called Mont Real or Mons Regalis. Conquered in 1189 by Saladin, it was restored in the 14th century by the Arabs, as witnessed by numerous inscriptions. Extant remains include the enclosing wall, a cistern and a well, as well as vestiges of a church and a small chapel with a baptistery dating to the Crusader period.

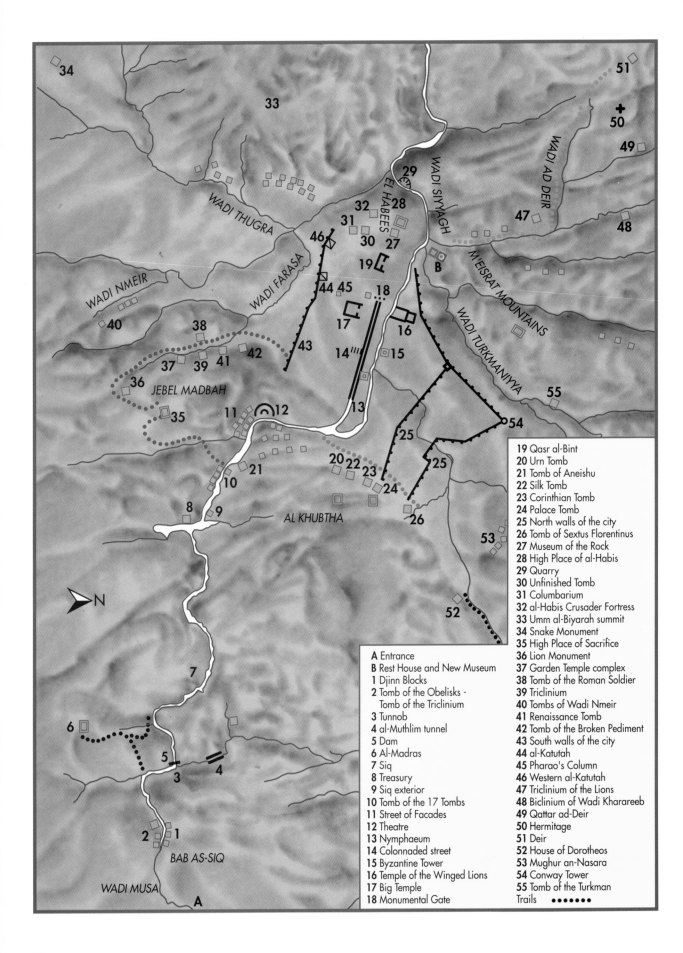

34

51

33

+
50

49

WADI AD DEIR

29

WADI SIYYAGH

32 28

EL HABEES

47

48

WADI THUGRA

31

30 27

46

19

B

M'EISRAT MOUNTAINS

WADI FARASA

44 45

18

WADI NMEIR

40

17

16

38

42

WADI TURKMANIYYA

43

14''''

15

55

37 39 41

JEBEL MADBAH

13

36

54

35

11   12

25

53

20 22 23

25

21

24

10

AL KHUBTHA

26

8   9

52

N

7

5
3   4

6

2   1

BAB AS-SIQ

WADI MUSA

A

| 19 Qasr al-Bint |
| 20 Urn Tomb |
| 21 Tomb of Aneishu |
| 22 Silk Tomb |
| 23 Corinthian Tomb |
| 24 Palace Tomb |
| 25 North walls of the city |
| 26 Tomb of Sextus Florentinus |
| 27 Museum of the Rock |
| 28 High Place of al-Habis |
| 29 Quarry |
| 30 Unfinished Tomb |
| 31 Columbarium |
| 32 al-Habis Crusader Fortress |
| 33 Umm al-Biyarah summit |
| 34 Snake Monument |
| 35 High Place of Sacrifice |
| 36 Lion Monument |
| 37 Garden Temple complex |
| 38 Tomb of the Roman Soldier |
| 39 Triclinium |
| 40 Tombs of Wadi Nmeir |
| 41 Renaissance Tomb |
| 42 Tomb of the Broken Pediment |
| 43 South walls of the city |
| 44 al-Katutah |
| 45 Pharao's Column |
| 46 Western al-Katutah |
| 47 Triclinium of the Lions |
| 48 Biclinium of Wadi Kharareeb |
| 49 Qattar ad-Deir |
| 50 Hermitage |
| 51 Deir |
| 52 House of Dorotheos |
| 53 Mughur an-Nasara |
| 54 Conway Tower |
| 55 Tomb of the Turkman |
| Trails ••••••• |

| A Entrance |
| B Rest House and New Museum |
| 1 Djinn Blocks |
| 2 Tomb of the Obelisks - Tomb of the Triclinium |
| 3 Tunnob |
| 4 al-Muthlim tunnel |
| 5 Dam |
| 6 Al-Madras |
| 7 Siq |
| 8 Treasury |
| 9 Siq exterior |
| 10 Tomb of the 17 Tombs |
| 11 Street of Facades |
| 12 Theatre |
| 13 Nymphaeum |
| 14 Colonnaded street |
| 15 Byzantine Tower |
| 16 Temple of the Winged Lions |
| 17 Big Temple |
| 18 Monumental Gate |

PETRA

There are few places in the world, especially those relatively easy to reach, whose impact on the visitor can be compared to the emotions aroused when, after rounding a bend in the narrow gorge called the Siq, he finds himself face to face with the tall facade of the "Treasury", the most famous monument in Petra. At every return the emotion presents itself anew, and one can vaguely imagine what the Anglo-Swiss explorer John Lewis Burckhardt must have felt in 1812, when, thanks to a stratagem, he became the first westerner to penetrate the ancient Nabataean capital whose existence and site were known only to the bedouins of the Jordanian desert, jealous guardians of this secret.

The area, naturally defended by a chain of high rock walls broken solely by the narrow passageway cut through by the waters of the Wadi Musa, offered a safe haven to numerous peoples in antiquity, from the Neolithic period on, and probably was the site of Sela, the Edomite capital cited in the Old Testament and in later works by Diodorus Siculus and Strabo. Relatively recent excavations have brought to light, on some of the hills near those subsequently chosen for the Nabataean settlement, numerous remains of dwellings as well as particularly interesting pieces of pottery. The Edomites, mentioned in the Bible as the descendents of Esau, were a northwestern Semitic people who appeared around the 13th century BC in the area between the Dead Sea and the gulf of Aqaba. Probably organized in a confederation of cities, for centuries they were constantly at war with the Israelites, although the latter never succeeded in completely subjugating them despite various crushing defeats. They were eventually driven from the area when a new Arab population of traders and caravaneers, the Nabataeans, moved in from the south. According to the Bible, the founding father was Nabath or Nabaioth, firstborn of Ishmael. It is however known that the Nabataeans spoke an Arab dialect written in Aramaic characters and that their principal deities were Dushara, a local divinity who may formerly have been Edomite (Duesh-Shara: he of Shara, the name of a mountain chain in the surroundings of Petra) and the goddess Allat ("the goddess"), whose cult was subsequently replaced by that of Al 'Uzza ("the powerful") and of Manat, protectress of the city. Dushara, initially depicted as a block of rock which was also the symbol of his dwelling, later took on the semblance of a bull, while Al'Uzza was shown as a lion. Other minor divinities included numerous deified sovereigns. Typical of the Nabataean religious culture were the so-called "high places", or open air altars for animal sacrifices located up high

on rocky ridges, and the "triclini", spaces in which the ceremonial meals that accompanied the religious or funerary rites were consumed. Originally nomads, the Nabataeans began to settle in the area of Petra around the 6th century BC, but only in late Hellenistic and in Roman times did their capital achieve the importance and wealth to which its monuments still bear witness. The origins of this wealth probably lay in an able policy of exploitation of the geographic site of the city, set along an obligatory route that joined the Arabian peninsula to the Syro-Anatolian area and Egypt; this permitted tolls to be exacted and meant that lodgings, water and provisions for the caravans that passed through could be furnished. Economical development soon led to the political hegemony over a vast area which expanded in the first century AD, with the sovereigns Obodas I and Aretas III, to include Amman and then Damascus, thus incrementing cultural ties with the Greek world. Petra's prosperity and independence continued under Aretas IV (8 BC-AD 40), but under his successors, who lacked the necessary diplomacy and efficiency, relations with Rome became tense and in AD 106 the Nabataean kingdom was annexed to the Roman empire, the result of a military campaign which permitted the Emperor Trajan to take over much of the Near East. Reduced to the rank of Roman province, the area began a slow decline when the trade routes shifted to the Euphrates, with the rapid growth in importance of cities such as Bosra, Dura Europos and Palmyra. Petra, however, modernized in line with Roman town planning principles, continued to enjoy a certain prosperity up to the middle of the 3rd century, when it stopped minting coins. The population was gradually converted to Christianity and the city became a bishop's seat. In the 6th century a violent earthquake led to the disappearance of many of the buildings of the Roman period, no longer dug into the rock but built on top, and may be why the city was abandoned. Various fortifications in the area, probably pre-existant, were remodelled and used in the period of the Crusades.

THE DJINN BLOCKS
AND THE TOMB OF THE OBELISKS

After leaving the built-up area of Wadi Musa (the "torrent of Moses"), which rose near the spring which is said to have miraculously sprung forth from the rock to offer refreshment to the Jews during their exodus from Egypt, the route moves along the ancient river bed, initially flanked by terraces and then by sandstone cliffs which draw closer and closer together. After reaching the government Rest House, one enters an area characterized on both sides by rounded dazzling white rock formations. The first monuments encountered are the three square towers, cut into the rock and known as the **Djinn Blocks** (the "Spirits"), three tombs probably erected in the 1st century BC, one of which still has the remains of a stepped pyramid at the top. The bedouins later mistook them for enormous water cisterns and rebaptized them Saharij (saahreej), an Arab term for cistern.

A bit further down, on the left side of the river bed, is the **Tomb of the Obelisks**, which a Greek and Nabataean inscription dates to the reign of Malichos II (AD 40-71). It is the first example of the imposing rock-cut structures which characterize the magic landscape of Petra. Usually, only the facade emerges from the rock wall, decorated in this case with elements of oriental, above all Egyptian, derivation, fused with others of clear Hellenistic matrix. The tomb is subdivided into two parts: the upper one, the actual Tomb of the Obelisks, has four pyramidal obelisks, an element typical of the Nabataean tombs, and probably derived from Egypt. The lower part, a few decades later and also known as the **Tomb of the Triclinium** after the benches set on three sides of the central chamber, is articulated by a double order, surmounted in both cases by a pediment, almost as if to create the illusion from a distance of two different buildings, with a perspective effect similar to that of Roman painting of the so-called "second style".

The Djinn Blocks, three square towers hewn out of the rock.

The Tomb of the Obelisks and the Tomb of the Triclinium.

The best way to get to the Siq is on horseback.

THE SIQ

About 300 m. south of the Tomb of the Obelisks is the Bab as-Siq, a narrow passageway that cuts through the striking sandstone cliffs tinted rose, yellow and grey blue. The result of a natural calamity which split the mountain, the Siq is about 2 km. long and also follows the dry bed of the torrent Musa, deviated by the Nabataeans to permit access to the city throughout the year. A dam has been built next to the cleft which constitutes the entrance to the Siq, to prevent flash floods which might endanger the lives of the tourists. This modern piece of hydraulic engineering replaces a similar one made by the Nabataeans and which was connected to the group of obelisks found in a good state of preservation during the recent work. The Nabataeans also dug a canal into the rock which brought water from the torrent into Petra; traces of this channel, which ran parallel to the Siq at a height of about 2 meters, are visible where the rock wall has been eroded. Not far from the dam are the ruins of the Triumphal Arch, still intact at the end of the last century. Only scarse vestiges of the original paving of the road remain along the Siq, and many of the decorative elements which marked the route-such as bas-reliefs and votive niches are often so badly eroded they can barely be distinguished.

Above, left, two pictures of the Siq and, below, a votive niche. On the right the majestic facade of the so-called Treasury, at the exit of the Siq.

The facade of the Treasury and the cleft in the rock which leads to the Siq.

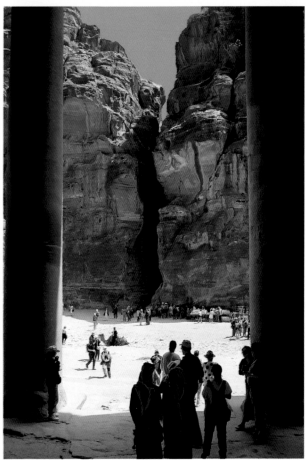

THE TREASURY

The tortuous path of the Siq continues, at times widening out or suddenly narrowing, and it is after a particularly narrow stretch that suddenly, after a curve, the majestic facade of the so- called **Treasury** (al-Khaznah) rises up. The facade, deeply excavated into the high rock wall right across from the exit from the Siq, is particularly striking in its proportions (about 40 m. high and 28 m. wide), the exceptional state of preservation of the stone, better protected there than elsewhere from erosion by the wind, the harmonious architectural composition of clear Hellenistic derivation, as well as the warm rose colour the excavated part has taken on, sharply contrasting with the browner tones of the intact surfaces of rock. The facade of the building is quite complex, with a highly elaborate double Corinthian order. The lower part consists of a six-columned pronaos surmounted by a tringular pediment: high reliefs now hard to decipher are set into the two blind intercolumniations at the sides. The upper part instead presents a central tholos, in other words a circular temple surmounted by a conical roof,

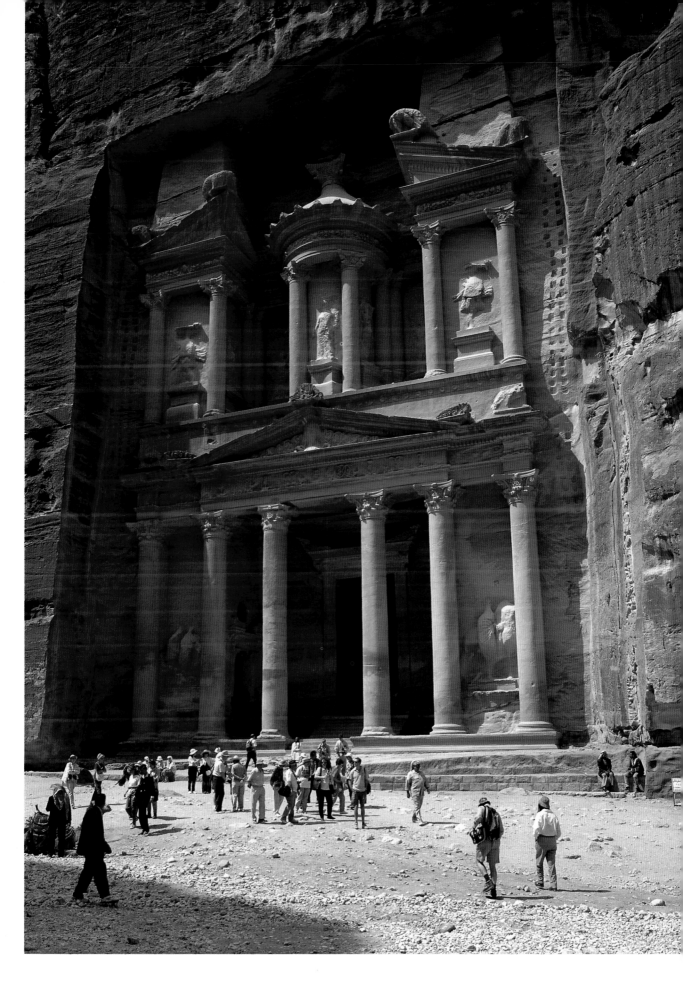

flanked by two lateral wings which repeat the blind intercolumnations of the lower order and are in turn topped by a half pediment; an identical frieze connects the architraves of the lateral wings and the tholos. It was the unusual shape of the latter which gave rise to the legend that the building contained the hidden treasure of a pharaoh; the signs left by the rifle shots fired by the Bedouins in their attempt to pierce the tholos bear witness to the belief in this legend among the local populations. The actual function (tomb, temple or royal mausoleum?) of this spectacular monument is in any case controversial, as is the period in which it was built, conjectures ranging from the reign of Aretas III (84-56 BC) to that of the Emperor Hadrian (AD 117-138).

Interior of the Treasury cut into the rock and details of the facade.

*Right above, the Tomb of the 17 Tombs.
Below, the "Street of Facades".*

Two pictures of the Theatre and, on the right, the Urn Tomb.

THEATRE
AND URN TOMB

To the right of the Treasury the ravine progressively widens, forming a natural arena in which are visible on the right the so- called **Tomb of the 17 Tombs**, a monument deeply excavated into the rock with 14 floor tombs inside, and another three on the back wall of the inner hall. Then come numerous tombs in Assyrian style, arrranged on various levels, the reason why this stretch of the so-called Outer Siq is called the "**Street of Facades**". The **Theatre** is located on the left. Excavated entirely out of the mountain in the 1st century AD, it consists of 33 tiers which can accommodate around 3000 spectators.

On the rock wall northeast of the Theatre, a series of splendid royal tombs are visible, dating to between the 1st and 2nd centuries of our epoch. The **Urn Tomb**, probably made for king Malichos II around 70 AD, is striking in the height and depth of the excavation work. The facade consists of a porch with four attached columns, with a trabeation on top, a very eroded attic, a second trabeation and a triangu-

lar pediment with a frieze on top and an urn. The tomb is preceded by a terrace flanked by a colonnade, sustained and at the same time made accessible by a ramp on arcading built in masonry and partially restored. The main inner hall, enormous in size, was transformed into a church in the middle of the 5th century.

Immediately to the left of the preceding tomb is the **Silk Tomb**. Extremely eroded by atmospheric agents, a series of four attached half columns can be barely made out on the facade, while the name comes from the blue, white, yellow and bright red striations on the horizontal bands of sandstone which recall watered silk. Further on is the evocative **Corinthian Tomb**: the general layout of the facade is very close to that of the Treasury, but the structure is not as well preserved.

Left, two details of the facade of the Urn Tomb and, below, the rock-cut interior with its fascinating colours.

Right, the Silk Tomb; below, the Corinthian Tomb.

Above, the Palace Tomb; below, the Tomb of Sextus Florentinus.

Right above, the Tomb of the Roman Soldier and the Tomb of the Broken Pediment. Below, the Triclinium.

The building immediately to the north, known as the **Palace Tomb**, with its facade arranged on three levels, is one of the most imposing monuments of the city. The two lower orders are as usual dug into the rock wall: the first has four doors - surmounted by pediments and framed by attached Nabataean columns - which lead to a single hypogeum; the second, considerably lower, is decorated with a series of half columns that are particularly close together. Very little remains of the third order, originally built in masonry. Moving northeast, we find the harmonious but damaged **Tomb of Sextus Florentinus**, a Roman proconsol of Arabia, probably erected by his son around AD 130.

THE SOUTHWEST AREA

Another group of interesting monuments is to be found in the area southwest of the Treasury, which can be reached thanks to the ascent on the **Jebel Attuf**. One of the most interesting is the **Tomb of the Roman Soldier**, a mausoleum in Hellenistic style which takes its name from the high reliefs on the facade, in which the deceased is shown wearing a cuirass. Particularly haunting is the **Triclinium** associated with this tomb, set opposite but without a facade. Extremely spacious, and with a sophisticated decoration in which attached half columns alternate with rectangular niches, this room is dug into a reddish-mauve rock striated with silver grey. About a third of the way up is the so-called **Lion Monument**, in which a bas-relief depicting this animal, the symbol of the goddess Al'Uzza, served as a fountain for pilgrims thanks to the water which was chanelled to gush from his mouth.

Top to bottom: Lion Monument; two pictures of the High Place of Sacrifice and an obelisk.

Right, two shots of the tombs seen from the lower city.

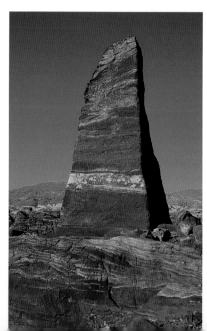

Above, the Monumental Gate; below, the Temple of the Winged Lions.

The ascent ends in the area of the so-called **High Place of Sacrifice**, located at a height of over a thousand metres. Of interest in addition to the sanctuary, probably of Edomite origins and later rebuilt by the Nabataeans, the site is outstanding for the magnificient view, which takes in the entire area of Petra and the surrounding mountains. In the south zone of the same rocky crest two obelisks can be seen, about thirty metres from each other and about 6 metres high, dug in a single block from the rock on which they rise: it is highly likely that they symbolize Dushara and Al'Uzza, the principal Nabataean divinities.

THE LOWER CITY

North of the Theatre, the outer Siq continues along the bed of the torrent of Moses and then turns left: it is in this area that the Roman town planning interventions are concentrated. The street which was once the principle artery of the Nabataean capital was carefully paved, endowed with public buildings such as a Nymphaeum, various markets and a bathing establishment, as well as columned porticoes and a **Monumental Gate**. Despite the fact that much of the gate is missing, it is still one of the best

Above, panorama of the lower city, with the Qasr Bint Firawn (Palace of the Pharaoh's Daughter) and a view of the interior in the photo below.

preserved structures, together with two Nabataean temples probably built between the 1st century BC and the 1st century AD. The first, set on the right side of the Colonnaded Street at the height of the Monumental Gate, is known as the **Temple of the Winged Lions** because of the decoration of the capitals which terminate in volutes of this shape. The holy building was probably dedicated to Atargatis, a female divinity assimilated to Venus who in the late Nabataean period took the place of Al' Uzza, and asorbed the symbolism.

The second Nabataean temple, known as **Qasr al-Bint**, or also as **Qasr Bint Firawn**, or "Palace of the Pharaoh's Daughter", stands on the left side of the street and is preceded by a spacious temenos, a sacred enclosure in which numerous finds of considerable interest were uncovered in the course of excavations. Although called "Palace", the Qasr al-Bint was really a temple consecrated to Dushara. As it is now, it is the only Nabataean building in Petra relatively well preserved that was entirely built and not dug out of the rock. Attributed to the reign of Obodas III and perhaps completed under Aretas IV at the beginning of our era, the building presents the remains of a vast portico with columns in antis. Entrance to a spacious cella is through an arch still miraculously standing in the back wall. In the thick side walls there was room for the stairs that led to the roof-terrace, which was also used in occasion of specific religious rites.

THE MUSEUM OF THE ROCK

A flight of stairs leads to a terrace in front of the **Museum of the Rock** with a fascinating view of the sea of ruins. The first museum created in Petra, it is housed inside a room dug out of the rock wall north of the lower city whose original function is unknown. A fine bearded head, probably a Roman copy of a Hellenistic original depicting Zeus, is set in a window above the entrance. Next to the door is a headless statue of Hercules, found in the Theatre area. The numerous fragments of Roman copies of Greek statues on exhibition here furnish an idea of the high level of culture achieved in the city where the population delighted in surrounding itself with finely made objects and was brought up in the classic taste of Greco-Roman culture. While the sculptures were probably imported - in fact no trace of a local re-elaboration exists, not even in a provincial style as is encountered in other Near Eastern localities - the refined painted pottery found in Petra was certainly produced locally, to which the remains of kilns discovered not far from the ancient Rest House bear witness. On the other hand the Edomites were skilled potters, and in a certain sense the bedouins now settled in the area also try to keep up the local tradition by making small clay objects in ancient forms, which they may sell as originals but at prices that are obviously too low. Others patiently fill small transparent bottles with coloured sand, creating imaginary landscapes, or gather fragments of the rock of Petra, with its typical varicolored striations, which they then offer to the tourist.

The head of Zeus above the entrance to the Museum of the Rock; below, two views of the museum interior.

Vendors of typical objects of bedouin crafts.

The road that leads to the Deir; below, the Tomb or Triclinium
of the Lions.

At the right, two fascinating pictures of the Deir (monastery).

THE DEIR

There is no question but that, together with the Treasury, this is one of the two most striking monuments in Petra. It is not all that easy to reach, but the splendid landscape through which one passes more than makes up for the effort. In the first stretch of the route which begins north of the Museum and then moves northwest, the **Tomb** or **Triclinium of the Lions** is encountered in a narrow ravine. The name derives from the lions in bas-relief on either side of the entrance. The decorative layout, which time has by now cancelled, was composed of attached pilasters with floral capitals, over which was an architrave with an elaborate frieze consisting of Medusa heads, triglyphs and disks, topped by a triangular pediment. Another half hour of climbing leads to the imposing monument known as **Deir**, or "Monastery". It might have been a temple dedicated to the deified king Obodas, created during the reign of the last Nabataean sovereign, Rabel II, at the end of the 1st century AD. The building, preceded by a large level space once certainly essential for the performance of the religious ceremonies, is entirely dug into the rock wall behind and contains an enormous inner room. The layout of the facade recalls that of the Treasury, although the proportions are

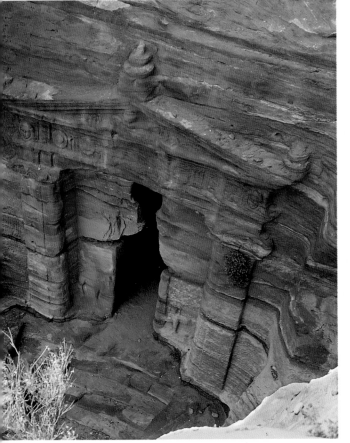

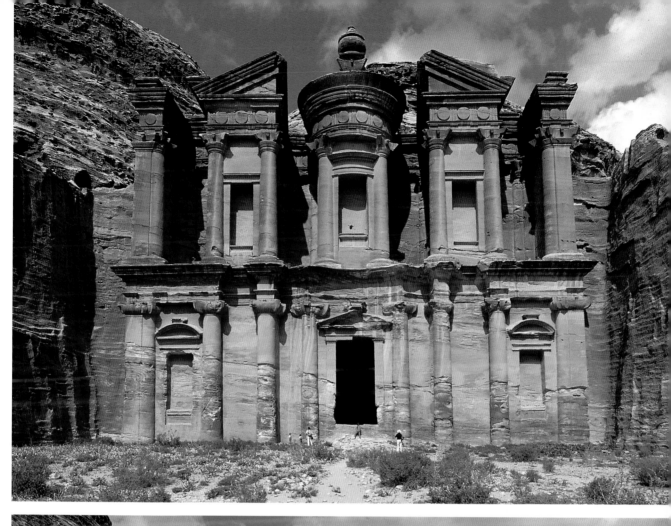

not the same, its width being greater than its height, about 50 m. by 40 m., and the lower order therefore differs. Compact, it contains only the central opening and two side niches, articulated by eight half columns set at varying distances so as to tie in with the upper order, here too characterized by a central tholos topped by an urn and flanked by two side wings over which is a broken half pediment, and with two narrow wings to respect the alignment with the lower part. The allover result is that of a lively architecture in which the rhythm of full and empty spaces, together with the strongly projecting cornices and stylized capitals, determine dramatic effects of light and dark and fully justify the definition "late antique Baroque".

THE NEW MUSEUM

This second museum, recently opened in an expressly built structure, provides an even more complete view of the objects of art and daily use which were part of the city's heritage. Many of the finds of various periods relating to the area of Petra which had previously been on exhibit in the Archaeological Museum of Amman or in the area in front of the Museum of the Rock have been transferred to this museum. One of the most famous pieces is the anthropomorphic idol in yellow sandstone found in the Temple of the Winged Lions, a rectangular stela with an inscription at the base and with a face with highly stylized features.

Above, the complex of the new Rest House and the New Museum. Below, the stela depicting an anthropomorphic idol and one of the rooms in the museum.

Right above, a winged lion and, below, a few decorative elements found in the area of Petra.

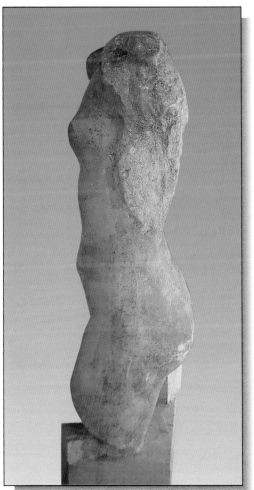

Above, the Columbarium; below, the Pharaoh's Column.

COLUMBARIUM AND THE PHARAOH'S COLUMN

Another excursion into the area immediately west of the lower city leads to the height of al-Habis, once presumably the site of the city's acropolis. To be found here are the remains of an open-air sacrificial area, of a triclinium, as well as of a Crusader fort, perhaps reused by the Arabs in the 13th century. In the first part of the route a decidedly unusual monument is encountered: the so-called **Columbarium**. This building, once more dug into the rock wall, has a myriad of small niches both on the facade and in the spacious inner hall, which were meant for the ashes of the deceased.

Moving in a southeast direction instead, towards the ridge of Attuf, the vestiges of a Nabataean construction and of a palace are encountered. The only extant element of the palace, probably part of a portico, is known as the **Pharaoh's Column**.

The brilliant colours of the sandstone eroded by time lend Petra its characteristic aspect.

It cannot be denied that much of Petra's charm derives from the patient excavations man has carried out in the course of the centuries, in an attempt to "tame" the naturally harsh aspect of the area's rock walls, turning it into an architecturally balanced "humanized" landscape. Even so the efforts made by nature to reappropriate itself of what was originally hers is just as striking, maintaining the allover aesthetic value of the site.

For every cornice, capital or pediment eroded by the fragments of wind-born sand, there are large areas of sandstone with fascinating striations in many shapes and colours - bright red, golden yellow, salmon, grey, white, and even a mauve which tends to blue - which become in turn still another feature of the city. This effect, almost absent where the harder surface strata of the rock were never touched, is produced only on those parts in which the soft sandstone had been uncovered, in a process begun by man but continued just as brilliantly by nature.

A bedouin tent set in a rocky landscape whose fantastic shapes evoke modern buildings, in the area of Little Petra.

Right, a few buildings in Little Petra.

LITTLE PETRA

A suburb a few kilometres north of the great Nabataean centre is known as Little Petra. In addition to its origins, it shares with the former the presence of a narrow entrance ravine - called as- Siq al-Barid - and buildings dug out of the rock. Nearby is the Neolithic village of El-Beida, with traces of a civilization similar to that of Jerico (ca. 7000 B.C.).

The pictures on these and the following pages were taken in a desert of Wadi Rum.
Russet rocks with graffiti; camels and off-road vehicles now travel through the red desert for a fascinating visit to the sites made famous by the exploits of Lawrence of Arabia.

WADI RUM

Rock formations and a fine sand of unusual colour which ranges from deep yellow to dark red constitute the principal features of the **desert of Wadi Rum**, located about a hundred kilometres south of Petra, in an area whose geological structure is similar to that of the rock walls of the Nabataean capital. While in the latter the extraordinarily beautiful views have been created above all by the patient work of man, in Wadi Rum it is the wind that throughout the millennia has eroded the rocks, thus creating the picturesque landscapes which have been attracting tourists of all countries for decades, and which were made famous by the film *Lawrence of Arabia*, when the shots on location were in part taken here. Obviously one needs an off-road vehicle and an expert guide - both of which can be found at the government Rest House - to venture into the vast stretches of reddish sand, from which rise rocks in

strange shapes and colours which seem to change continually as one moves along. Already inhabited in prehistoric times, as witnessed by the finds of stone tools dating to the Paleolithic and Neolithic periods, this great valley was roamed for millennia by hunters and nomads, who left interesting traces of their passage. Most of these are graffiti, rupestral engravings both on the rocks and rock walls and inside natural caves, presumably ranging in time from the 4th millennium BC up almost to the present. There are depictions of hunting scenes with bow and arrow, with stylized but lively figures of men and animals, and inscriptions in Tamudic (a writing that appeared in the 7th cent. BC), Nabataean, and Arab. The most recent engravings even show guns and automobiles and were made by the bedouins of today, who are rapidly adopting modern technology

AQABA

The far-distant origins of the city of Aqaba, after which the gulf at the end of the eastern branch of the Red Sea is named, go back to a settlement dating to several millennia before our era. The geographical location, of vital importance in connecting the coasts of the Arabian peninsula and the Mediterranean area, always meant that the spot was of particular interest to various peoples and dynasties, who engaged in bitter battles for possession of the site. Interesting traces of the early medieval Islamic city called Ila or Ayla have been brought to light in the course of recent excavations, at the center of the seaside promenade where visitors are welcome. The finds from this area - principally pottery and objects of use dating to the Umayyad, Abbasid and Fatimid periods (7th-12th centuries) - are at present on exhibit in the small archaeological Museum housed inside the **Castle**. Erected by the Mamluke sultan Khanso al-Ghuri at the beginning of the 16th century in an area where the citadel of Ila once stood, the exterior of the castle seems forbidding but

The entrance and interior, restored, of the famous Castle of Aqaba; right, the modern city and the new mosque.

125

inside is a pleasant court, on which the various rooms open. In addition to serving as defense, in times of peace, the building was meant to offer hospitality to pilgrims on their way to the Mecca.

Today Aqaba is a lively tourist centre and an active port (the only one in Jordan). The relatively stable temperature means that bathing in the clear waters of the Red Sea is possible practically all year long. With a wealth of marine flora and fauna that has disappeared elsewhere, it is a popular site for scuba diving, and it is advisable to contact one of the numerous European sub-acqua clubs which have their headquarters in the city and are also equipped with glass-bottomed boats so that the coral reef can be seen from the surface. Hotel facilities in the deluxe category are also available, with western comforts in a pleasantly exotic atmosphere.

The lovely beaches of Aqaba overlook the crystal-clear waters of the Red Sea.

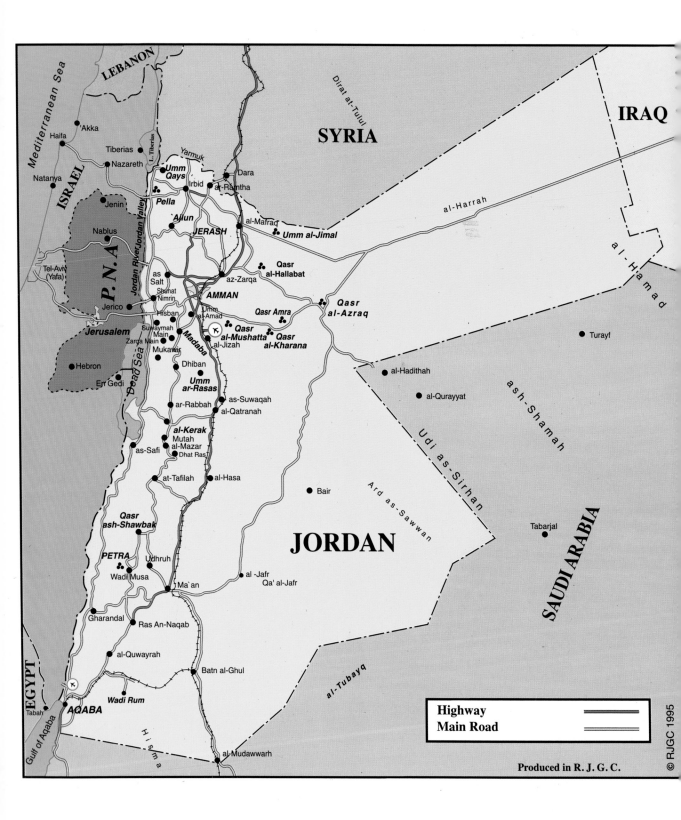

Highway

Main Road

© RJGC 1995

Produced in R. J. G. C.